Werner Blaser

POST TOWER

HELMUT JAHN
WERNER SOBEK
MATTHIAS SCHULER

Birkhäuser – Publishers for Architecture
Birkhäuser – Verlag für Architektur
Basel · Boston · Berlin

Translation from German into English: William Martin, Berlin
Translation of Helmut Jahn's Introduction from English into German: Jutta Amri, Trier

A CIP catalogue record for this book is available from the Library of
Congress, Washington D.C., USA.

Bibliographic information published by Die Deutsche Bibliothek
Die Deutsche Bibliothek lists this publication in the Deutsche Nationalbibliografie; detailed
bibliographic data is available in the internet at http://dnb.ddb.de.

© 2004 Birkhäuser – Publishers for Architecture, P.O. Box 133, CH-4010 Basel, Switzerland.
Member of Springer Science+Buisness Media

Printed on acid-free paper produced from chlorine-free pulp. TCF ∞

Layout: Werner Blaser and Keith H. Palmer
Litho and typography: Photolitho Sturm AG, Muttenz

Printed in Germany

ISBN 3-7643-6990-6

9 8 7 6 5 4 3   http://www.birkhauser.ch

Inhaltsverzeichnis

Contents

Geleitwort

Der Post Tower, ein Symbol für die Innovationsfreude der Stadt Bonn und des Konzerns

Mit der Errichtung des Post Towers haben wir ein neues Kapitel in der Geschichte von Deutsche Post World Net aufgeschlagen.

Auf dem erfolgreichen Weg von einer nationalen Behörde zu einem globalen Dienstleistungskonzern sollte unser Haus Symbol des Wandels und Kommunikationsplattform für neue Ideen und Entwicklungen sein. Wir wollten zeigen, was im Gebäude passiert, und die Offenheit der Unternehmenskultur des weltweit agierenden Logistikkonzerns Deutsche Post World Net demonstrieren.

Unsere Vision war deshalb ein Gebäude von großer Transparenz und Flexibilität. Die Architektur sollte auch die Dynamik und Modernität des Unternehmens darstellen.

Mit konstruktiver Unterstützung der Stadt Bonn haben wir die planungsrechtlichen Voraussetzungen für unsere Ziele in kurzer Zeit umsetzen können. Um die hohen Ansprüche an Form und Funktion des Gebäudes sicherzustellen, wurde ein internationaler Wettbewerb ausgelobt. Mit Helmut Jahn haben wir unseren idealen Architekten und ein Konzept für ein architektonisches Highlight gefunden.

Ausschlaggebend für die Entscheidung für Jahn war, dass er unser Verständnis von modernen Arbeitsprozessen und effizienten Organisationsstrukturen am innovativsten umgesetzt hat. Unter Berücksichtigung ökologischer und ökonomischer Gesichtspunkte sind hier Arbeitsplatzbedingungen geschaffen, die in räumlicher Ausprägung und dem Einsatz intelligenter Technik neue Maßstäbe setzen.

Der Post Tower ist nicht nur Ergebnis modernster Architekturkunst, sondern setzt gleichzeitig ein deutliches Signal in Richtung einer erfolgreichen Zukunft des Konzerns Deutsche Post World Net.

Dr. Hans-Dieter Petram   Franz Werner Nolte
Vorstand   Geschäftsführer
Deutsche Post World Net   Deutsche Post Bauen GmbH

Foreword

The Deutsche Post Tower: A Symbol of Bonn's and the Deutsche Post's Enthusiasm for Innovation

With the building of the Post Tower, a new chapter has been opened in the history of Deutsche Post World Net. As we made a successful transition from a national enterprise to a global service corporation, we wanted our headquarters to be a symbol of transformation and a platform for communicating new ideas and developments. Our plan was to show what takes place inside the building and to demonstrate the openness with which this international logistics corporation, Deutsche Post World Net, does business.

So we envisioned a building of maximum transparency and flexibility. The design similarly represents the company's inherent dynamism and modernity.

The City of Bonn's constructive support enabled us to establish our project's compliance with planning laws in very short time. In order to meet our high expectations for the building's form and function, we held an international competition. In Helmut Jahn we found an ideal architect for the project and a concept for a true architectural feat.

The deciding factor in choosing Jahn was his superior innovation in implementing our understanding of modern work procedures and efficient organization structures. Taking into account both ecological and economic perspectives, he has created working conditions here that set new standards in their expression of space and their incorporation of intelligent technology.

The Post Tower represents the pinnacle of modern architectural design, and at the same time sends a clear signal to the future – a future of success for the Deutsche Post World Net corporation.

Dr. Hans-Dieter Petram
Chairman of the Board
Deutsche Post World Net

Franz Werner Nolte
Chief Executive Officer
Deutsche Post Bauen GmbH

Post Tower, Bonn: Einführung von Helmut Jahn

Konzept:

1997 schrieb die Deutsche Post einen öffentlichen Wettbewerb für den Bau ihrer neuen Hauptverwaltung aus. Unser Entwurf wurde nach mehreren Stufen ausgewählt. Fertigstellung des Baus war im Frühjahr 2003.

Es war ausdrückliche Zielvorgabe des Bauherrn, dass dieses Bauwerk die progressive Firmenpolitik des heute privat geführten Unternehmens, bekannt als Deutsche Post World Net, zum Ausdruck bringt.

In Komposition mit Egon Eiermanns Gebäude «Langer Eugen» und Joachim Schürmanns «Deutscher Welle» stellt der Post Tower das Bindeglied zwischen der Stadt und dem Park entlang des Rheinufers dar. Diese Aspekte nahmen Einfluss auf die Gebäudeform und führten zu der behutsamen und aerodynamischen Spaltung der versetzten Halbellipsen. Sie bestimmten ebenfalls das Zirkulations-Diagramm, welches öffentlichen Raum zwischen die Gebäudehälften fädelt und mit großzügigen Treppen und Rampen den Park mit der oberen Rhein-Terrasse verbindet.

Der Post Tower stellt eine neue Typologie für ein Bürohochhaus dar. Die nördlichen und südlichen Halbellipsen werden durch einen 7,20 m breiten Raum voneinander getrennt. Glasböden unterteilen diesen Zwischenraum in neungeschossige Skygärten, die als Kommunikationsbereiche dienen. Oben grenzt ein zweigeschossiger Raum und ein Penthouse mit glasgefasster Terrasse die Bereiche der Geschäftsleitung ab. Zwei Gruppen von Aufzügen erschließen alle Geschosse, ermöglichen den Blick auf Stadt und Landschaft und vermitteln ein dramatisches Erlebnis von Bewegung: als Raum, als Freude und als Geschwindigkeit. Im Sockelgebäude sind Cafeteria, Sitzungs- und Konferenzeinrichtungen untergebracht.

Der Post Tower ist der Ausdruck einer neuen Bauweise. Seine Komponenten sind minimal, integrieren das Engineering und erfüllen somit gleichzeitig architektonische, konstruktive und mechanische Zwecke. Das ästhetische Erscheinungsbild des Turms ist das Ergebnis der koordinierten Gesamtheit dieser Systeme und Komponenten. Die Zielsetzung besteht darin, dass Perfektion nur dann erreicht wird, wenn nichts mehr weggelassen werden kann. Das Resultat sind Transparenz, Ökologie und Komfort der Nutzers.

Hülle:

Die Fassade ist anpassungsfähig und steuerbar. Sie kontrolliert das Raumklima durch Design und nicht durch zusätzliche technische Ausstattung. Das Hauptkonzept liegt in natürlicher Belüftung und Tageslicht und der damit verbundenen Sonnenenergie sowie der elektronischen Steuerung beider. So wird die Fassade zum Vermittler zwischen den äußeren Bedingungen und der gewünschten Behaglichkeit der Nutzer im Inneren. Größtmöglicher Komfort wird mit minimaler technischer Ausstattung erreicht. Das Ziel ist die Annäherung an die wunderbare biologische Anpassungsfähigkeit der menschlichen Haut.

Um die natürlichen Ressourcen zu maximieren und die technische Ausstattung auf ein Mindestmaß zu reduzieren, entschieden wir uns für eine zweischalige Fassadenkonstruktion. Die voll verglasten inneren und äußeren Hüllen ermöglichen die natürliche Belüftung und bilden Wind-, Regen-, und Lärmschutz. Hinter den äußeren Schalen sind die Sonnenschutzlamellen angebracht. Die Klimaregulierung erfolgt durch Luftansaugung aus dem kontrollierten Luftraum zwischen den Schalen durch die Fenster oder durch einen speziellen Anschluss am Deckenrand. Von dort wird die Luft durch einen Konvektor im Doppelboden erwärmt oder gekühlt und nach dem Quellluftprinzip verteilt. Dieses System unterstützt das Grundsystem der Bauteilkühlung/Heizung, das in die Betondecken integriert ist. Während die Nordfassade durchgehend vertikal ist, wird die Südfassade aus Gründen der besseren natürlichen Luftzirkulation bei hohen Außentemperaturen schuppenartig geneigt. Regulierbare Lüftungsklappen werden zentral gesteuert.

Post Tower, Bonn: Introduction by Helmut Jahn

Concept:

In 1997 the Deutsche Post held an open competition for their new Corporate Center. After several stages our design was selected and completed by spring 2003.

It was the expressed goal of the client for the building to become a statement of progressive corporate policy for the privatized, former government-owned company, now known as Deutsche Post World Net.

The tower forms an ensemble together with Egon Eiermann's "Langer Eugen" and Joachim Schürmann's "Deutsche Welle", and marks the transition from the city to the park along the Rhine river. These aspects influenced the shape of the building and led to the soft and aerodynamic split and shifted half shells. They also determined the circulation diagram, which threads public space through the site between the buildings and connects with generous stairs and ramps the park with the upper terrace near the Rhine.

The Post Tower represents a new typology for an office tower. The north and south half shells are separated by 7.2 m wide spaces, which are divided by glass floors into nine-story skygardens, which serve as communication floors. At the top, a two-story space and a penthouse with a screened roof terrace define the executive areas. Two groups of glass elevators serve all floors, allow views of the city and the landscape and give a dramatic experience of movement and motion: as space, as elation, as speed. The low building contains cafeteria, meeting and conference facilities.

The Post Tower makes a statement for a new way of building. Its components are minimal, integrated with engineering and thus serve architectural, structural and mechanical purposes at once. Its aesthetic and appearance derives from the coordinated whole of these systems and components. The goal is that perfection can only be achieved if nothing can be taken away. Transparency, ecology and user comfort are the resulting benefits.

Enclosure:

The facade is adaptable and switchable. It controls its environment by design and not through additional technical equipment. Natural ventilation, daylight with its connected solar energy and their intelligent control are the main strategies. They mediate between the external conditions and the desired internal comfort of the users. Comfort is maximized and technical equipment is reduced. The goal is to approximate with the facade the wonderful adaptability of the biological human skin.

In order to maximize the natural resources and minimize technical equipment, we opted for a twin shell facade. The fully glazed outer and inner glass shells enable natural ventilation, protection from noise, rain and wind, and allow for placement of shades behind the outer-shells. For conditioning, air is taken from the controlled airspace between the shells through the windows or a special detail at the slab edge, heated or cooled by a convector in the raised floor and distributed from there along the displacement principle. This system supports the basic heating and cooling through the integrated piping system in the coffered exposed concrete slabs.

At the south face the facade is shingled to allow for better natural airflow at hot outside temperatures. The outer shell of the north face is straight. Operable flaps at the gaps of the shingles and the straight north wall allow for central control.

The roof of the base building and the penthouse is covered with a cellular panel system. It acts as roofing, insulation, acoustic barrier, and accommodates ventilation and admits daylight. Over the lifetime of the building as use demands or new technologies are available, this system can be changed or adapted with minimal effort or disruption.

Das Dach des Sockelgebäudes und das Penthousedach sind mit einem zellulären Paneelsystem bedeckt. Es dient als Dacheindeckung, Dämmung, Lärmschutz und ermöglicht Belüftung und den Einfall von natürlichem Tageslicht. Je nach Nutzungsanforderungen oder neu vorhandenen Technologien ist dieses System im Laufe der Lebenszeit des Gebäudes mit geringem Aufwand austauschbar und anpassbar.

Innenraum:

Die Gestaltung des Innenraums erfolgte nach dem Standard der typisch deutschen Bürozellenplanung. Mit dem Entwurf eines speziellen Trennwandsystems mit klaren und transluzenten Oberflächen wurde die Zielvorgabe visueller Offenheit und Transparenz erreicht, die auch dem Bedürfnis der Nutzer nach Privatsphäre entgegenkommt.

Beleuchtung:

Die Behandlung von Licht und Lichtkunst als integrale Bestandteile der Architektur war eines der Hauptanliegen des Bauherrn und des Architekten. Deshalb war Yann Kersalé von Beginn ein wichtiger Mitarbeiter im Team. Kersalé bezeichnet sein Konzept als «Allégorie Trichromique». Die Lichtkunst beabsichtigt die Wahrnehmung des Gebäudes bei Nacht, indem sie die Schichten und Transparenz der Glasarchitektur sichtbar macht und ihr Substanz, Verbindung und ästhetischen Sinn verleiht. Zwischen Dämmerung und Sonnenaufgang vollzieht sich eine Lichtinszenierung, die mit dem Leben des Objekts verbunden ist. Die funktionelle Bürobeleuchtung und die Fassadenbeleuchtung variieren mit der Belegung des Gebäudes und führen zu dynamischen Farbvariationen, die zu virtuellen Zeitzeichen werden.

Tragwerk:

Die außerordentlichen Erwartungen in das Gebäude wurden auch durch den Einsatz fortschrittlicher und innovativer Lösungen sowohl im Bereich der tragenden Konstruktionen als auch in der Konstruktion der Fassaden erfüllt. Alle konstruktiven Teile wurden mit Hinblick auf größtmögliche Leichtigkeit, Transparenz und Klarheit geplant. Eine weitere Zielsetzung bestand im Erreichen einer Multifunktionalität der Bauelemente. Letztere kann beispielhaft an den Stahlbetondeckenplatten des Gebäudes erläutert werden. Diese Deckenplatten sind nicht nur lastabtragende Elemente, sondern sie werden auch von einem integrierten Rohrsystem zur Kühlung und Heizung der Bauteile durchzogen. Die Bauhöhen der Deckenplatten wurden auf ein Mindestmaß reduziert. Am Deckenrand, wo am Berührpunkt zwischen Fassade und Decke ein Maximum an Transparenz erreicht werden musste, laufen die Decken auf wenige Zentimeter Bauhöhe aus. Zur Verringerung des Eigengewichts wurden die Platten an ihrer Unterseite mit großen gewölbeartigen Ausnehmungen versehen. Diese Ausnehmungen mit ihren gekrümmten Oberflächen dienen gleichzeitig als Lichtreflektoren. Die Beleuchtungskörper selbst wurden speziell für das Gebäude entworfen und oberflächenbündig an den Rändern der Deckenausnehmungen integriert.

Die hohe Funktionalität aller Bauteile und die stete Suche nach dem Angemessenen und Einfachen bedeuteten eine umfassende integrale Planung, eine behutsame Detailplanung, streng vereinfachte Anschlussdetails mit hohem Wiederholungsgrad und die Verwendung der Materialien in ihren grundeigenen und charakteristischen Eigenschaften. Dies führte letztlich zu einem in sich schlüssigen, klaren und eleganten Erscheinungsbild, sowohl an den einzelnen Tragwerksteilen als auch an der Gesamtkonstruktion.

Die Hauptkonstruktion, also das Primärtragwerk, besteht eigentlich aus zwei Gebäuden mit der Grundrissform von Halbellipsen, die jeweils zwei Betonkerne und 19 Stahlverbundstützen besitzen. Die beiden «Teilgebäude» stehen auf einem gemeinsamen Kellerkasten. Sie sind im Bereich der Kerne mit zwei Reihen à fünf Auskreuzungen miteinander verbunden. Hierdurch entsteht ein sehr effektives und dennoch sehr transparentes Tragsystem. Zusätzlich wurden auf halber Gebäudehöhe im Bereich des Technikgeschosses Diagonalstäbe

Interior:

The interior had to follow the typical German standard of a cellular office layout. By designing a special glass partition system, which is now available on the market, the goals of visual openness and transparency have been achieved through clear and translucent surfaces, which also meet the need for privacy of the occupants.

Lighting:

A major goal of client and architect was the desire to treat lighting and lighting art as integral part of the architecture. Therefore, Yann Kersalé was an important member of the team from the beginning. Kersalé describes his concept as an Allégorie Trichromique. The intention of the light art is to create a perception of the building by night, which shows the layering and transparency of the glass-architecture and gives it substance, connection and aesthetic sense. From dusk to sunrise a scenario starts, which is connected with the Life of the Object. The functional office lighting and the facade lighting vary with the occupancy of the building and result in dynamic color variations, which become virtual signs of time.

Structure:

The extraordinary expectations for the building have been mirrored by advanced and innovative structural solutions for the structure and for the façade. All structural elements have been designed with a view to achieve maximum lightness, transparency and clarity. Another objective were multifunctional building components. The latter fact is exemplified by looking at the reinforced concrete slabs. These slabs do not only act as load bearing elements, they also show an integrated piping system for heating and cooling. The structural height of the slabs has been minimized as far as possible. Especially along the edges at the meeting point of facade and slab, a maximum of transparency had to be achieved; here the height of the slabs is merely a few centimetres. In order to minimize dead weight, the slabs are coffered. The curved surface of the coffers acts simultaneously as a light reflector. The light fixtures themselves have been specially designed for the building; they are integrated flush with the surface at the edges of the coffers.

The high functionality of all building components as well as the constant quest for the appropriate and the basic mean careful detailing, strictly simplified connection details with a high degree of repetition and a use of the materials which meets their basic and characteristic properties. In the end this led to a coherent, clear and elegant appearance, both in the individual components of the structure and in the whole building.

The main structure, i.e. the primary load-bearing structure, consists of two buildings. These buildings are, in plan view, half shells; they have each two concrete cores and 19 steel composite columns. The two buildings forming the main structure stand on a joint basement. Their concrete cores are linked by two rows of five X-bracings each. This leads to a very efficient, yet very transparent load-bearing structure. In addition, on the technical installations level halfway up the building, there are additional diagonal outriggers; these outriggers link the cores with the external support columns. This type of outrigger-structure combined with four interlocked cores leads to a further stiffening of the primary structure.

The facade is a perfect example of "Archi-Neering", i.e. the integration of architecture and engineering. On the one hand, the size of the glass panes used has been maximized; on the other hand, the size of the facade profiles has been minimized so as to render them hardly perceptible. Moreover, the outer skin of the facade is hung in portions of nine stories each. This made it possible to use more slender profiles (because this part of the structure is subject only to tension), to reduce joint sizes, and to simplify the detailing. The interior facades, which are facing the atrium, are equally fully glazed. The atrium itself is bridged by glazed steel bridges at each floor. The same glazed floor structure has been used in the skygardens.

angeordnet, die den Treppenhauskern mit den Randstützen verbinden. Dieses Outrigger-System in Kombination mit den verbundenen Kernen bewirkt eine weitere Versteifung der Primärkonstruktion.

Die Fassade ist ein schönes Beispiel für «Archi-Neering», die Integration von Architektur und Engineering. Einerseits wurden die verwendeten Glasfelder auf ein größtmögliches Maß maximiert, andererseits wurden die Tragprofile derart minimiert, dass man sie kaum noch wahrnimmt. Darüber hinaus wurde die äußere Fassadenhaut über jeweils neun Geschosse abgehängt; dies ermöglichte schlankere Profile infolge der ausschließlichen Zugbeanspruchung, reduzierte Fugengrößen und eine vereinfachte Detailausbildung. Die inneren, zum Atrium gerichteten Fassaden sind ebenfalls voll verglast. Das Atrium selbst wird auf jeder Etage über gläserne Brücken erschlossen. Das gleiche gläserne Fußbodensystem wurde bei den Skygärten angewandt.

Energiekonzept:

«Im Wind atmen», so lässt sich die ausgeglichene Luftbewegung durch die verschiedenen Fassadenschichten und -räume im neuen Post Tower in Bonn beschreiben. Sie basiert auf dem Prinzip der zweischaligen Fassade, das damit kein Zusatz ist, sondern die Grundlage des Komfort- und Energiekonzeptes bildet. Das Gebäude wird ganzjährig zu 100% über den Luftraum der Fassaden belüftet, und dies ohne Nutzung eines zentralen mechanischen Systems. Die typische Büroetage verwendet das Plenum der zweischaligen Fassade für die Luftansaugung und die innenliegenden Skygärten zur Abluftsammlung. Dies ermöglicht das Weglassen aller vertikalen Luftverteilungsschächte und trägt damit beträchtlich zur Effizienz des Gebäudes bei. Durch dieses dezentralisierte Klimatisierungssystem konnte ein zusätzliches Haustechnikgeschoss eingespart werden. All diese Einsparungen können für die erhöhten Kostenaufwendungen der komplexeren Fassadenaufbauten verwendet werden.

Der wind- und wettergeschützte Sonnen- und Blendschutz hinter der äußeren Glasschale ermöglicht größtmögliche Transparenz durch die Verwendung von eisenoxydarmem Glas und einer neutralen metallischen Beschichtung bei der inneren Isolierverglasung mit Argon- Füllung. Die Reduzierung der äußeren Strahlenbelastung und die Verringerung der inneren Wärmelasten durch eine tageslichtgesteuerte künstliche Beleuchtung erlaubt es, die Raumklimatisierung auf ein in den Stahlbetondeckenplatten integriertes Heiz- und Kühlsystem zu begrenzen. Dieses Rohrsystem ist über einen Wärmetauscher mit dem Grundwasser verbunden und sorgt damit für natürliche Kühlung ohne die Verwendung einer Kühlanlage.

Das Energie- und Komfortkonzept, welches mit Hilfe eines integrierten Entwurfskonzeptes entwickelt wurde, wird vom Verbraucher individuell mit Hinblick auf die Raumtemperatur, die Luftqualität und die Raumbeleuchtung gesteuert. Die Verwendung der Gebäudehülle als Luftverteiler ermöglicht die Reduzierung der technischen Gebäudeausstattung bei der Raumklimatisierung. Eine überzeugende Folge war der Gewinn von zusätzlichen 1000 m^2 Mietflächen. Das integrierte Komfortkonzept erlaubt die individuelle Regelung von Temperatur und Luftzufuhr in jedem Raum, selbst im Sommer, und dies ist nicht Standard für eine typische Büroumgebung. Es basiert grundsätzlich auf der Nutzung örtlich natürlich vorhandener Kältequellen wie Grundwasser und nächtliche Abkühlung. Mit der steuerbaren Außenhaut kann der Verbraucher im 40. Stockwerk selbst entscheiden, wann er sein Fenster öffnen möchte, und die Funktion des Sonnenschutzes ist sichergestellt. Ein Ergebnis des Zusammenwirkens von Außenhülle, Tragkonstruktion und Klimasystem des Gebäudes ist, dass sich der absehbare Energiebedarf dieses Gebäudes auf weniger als 100 kWh/m^{2}a für Heizung, Belüftung, Kühlung und künstliche Beleuchtung beläuft.

Energy Concept:

"Breathing in the wind" describes the balanced airflow through the different facade layers and spaces in the new Post Tower in Bonn. It is based on the twin-shell facade concept for the whole comfort and energy concept, but not as an add-on. 100% of the year the building is ventilated through the air space between the shells without using a central mechanical system. The typical office floor uses this space as the intake air distribution and the inner sky-gardens as exhaust collection, which allows eliminating all vertical air distribution shafts, a major aspect increasing the building's efficiency. In addition one mechanical floor is saved through this ventilation concept, using decentralized air intake units in the standard underfloor convectors. All these savings are transferred for covering the additional costs for the more complex facades.

The wind and weather protected shading device behind the outer single glass shell allows the glass to be kept as transparent as possible, using low iron glass and a neutral low-e coating for the inner double glazing with argon filling. Through this reduction of external loads and by minimizing the internal loads with daylight-controlled artificial lighting, the space conditioning can be limited to an integrated heating and cooling system in the concrete ceilings. This piping is via a heat exchanger connected to a ground-water well providing natural cooling without using a chiller.

The comfort and energy concept, which was developed in an integrated design approach is controlled by the individual user with regards to the space temperature, air quality and room illumination. The use of the building envelope for the air distribution allows the reduction of the technical building equipment for the space conditioning. Additional 1000 m² rental space were the convincing consequence. The integrated comfort concept allows an individual temperature and airflow control per room even in summer, which is not usual in a typical office environment. It is mainly based on the use of a local natural cooling source, like the ground water and night cooling. Through the controlled external skin, the user up to the 40th floor can decide when he wants to open his window, and the function of the shading is ensured. As a result of the collaboration of building envelope, building structure and building environmental system, the energy demand of this building is predicted to be less than 100 kWh/m²a for heating, ventilation, cooling and artificial lighting.

Außenraum
Konzept und Wirkung

Durch die Spaltung des Gebäudes wurde ein Tor von der Stadt zum Rhein und zum Siebengebirge geschaffen. Die Vollendung der städtebaulichen Gesamtkomposition ist gemeinsam mit dem «Schürmann-Bau» und dem «Langen Eugen» erreicht; der Post Tower akzentuiert einen punktförmigen, städtebaulichen Abschluss: ein Gebäude mit einem verbindenden, öffentlichen Charakter und Erlebniswert. Die überdachte, offene Passage vermittelt zwischen dem Vorplatz an der Kurt-Schumacher-Straße und dem Rheinauen Park. Läden und Restaurants aktivieren diesen Link.

Das formale und ästhetische Erscheinungsbild des Bürohochhauses ist eine gespaltene Ellipse mit vier gestapelten Skygärten, die sich zur Stadt Bonn und zum Rhein orientieren. Die Erfordernisse der Ingenieur-Kunst und der Technologie zwingen herkömmliche Materialien und Systeme zu neuen Grenzen. Das Hauptinteresse ist es nicht, High-Tech darzustellen, sondern die Leistung des Gebäudes zu verbessern. Die Form ist durch die Integration von Struktur und Materialien minimal und einprägsam. Keine Anpassung ist notwendig. Das Neue wird dramatisiert und kann so zum Wahrzeichen für die Deutsche Post World Net und die Stadt Bonn werden.

The Exterior
Design and Effect

The cleft in the building creates a gateway between the city and the Rhine river and the Siebengebirge mountain range. With the "Schürmann Building" and the "Langer Eugen," the total urban development composition was completed. The Post Tower accentuates a pointed terminus of the urban plan: a building with an inviting, open character and experiential value. The well-designed open passage forms a transition between a forecourt on Kurt-Schumacher-Strasse and Rheinauen Park. Shops and restaurants activate the link.
The office building's form and aesthetic is that of a divided half shell with four staggered skygardens oriented towards Bonn and the Rhine. The demands it placed on engineering technique and on technology itself have pushed conventional materials and systems to new limits. The primary motivation for this was not to demonstrate hi-tech achievements, but to enhance the building's capacities. Through the integration of structure and materials the form remains both minimal and memorable; it needs no adjustments. This dramatization of the new may thus become a hallmark of both the Deutsche Post World Net and the city of Bonn.

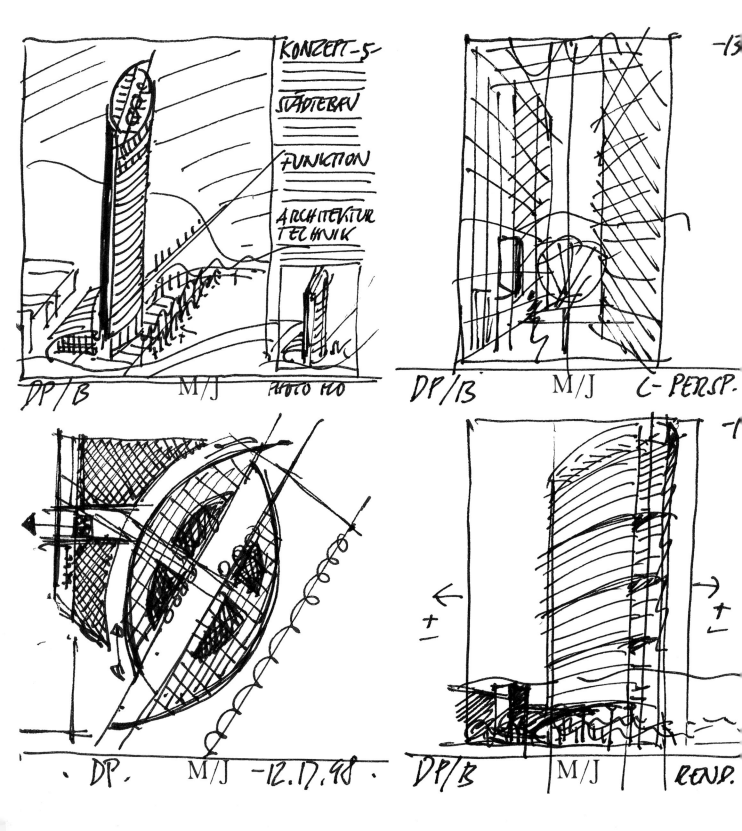

KONZEPT -5-

STÄDTEBAU

FUNKTION

ARCHITEKTUR
TECHNIK

DP/B   M/J   PHOTO H/O

DP/B   M/J   C-PERSP.   -13

. DP.   M/J -12.17.98 .

DP/B   M/J   REND.

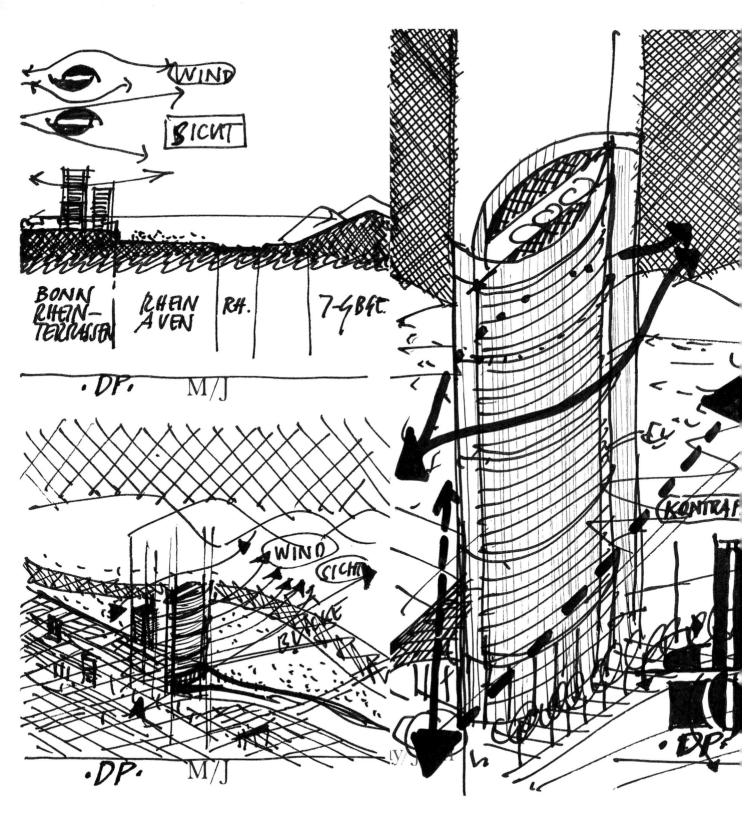

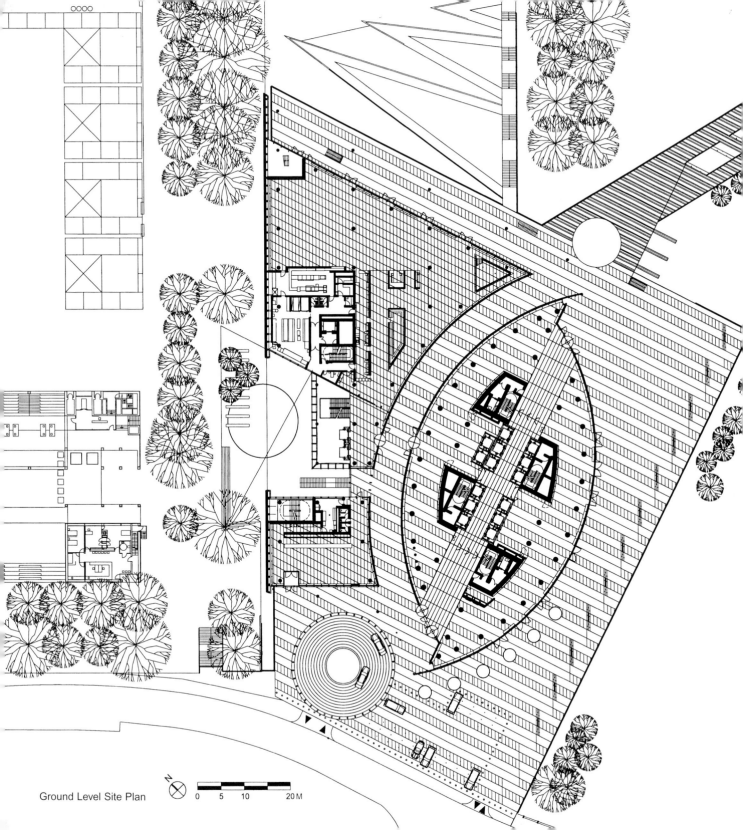

Ground Level Site Plan

N

0 5 10   20 M

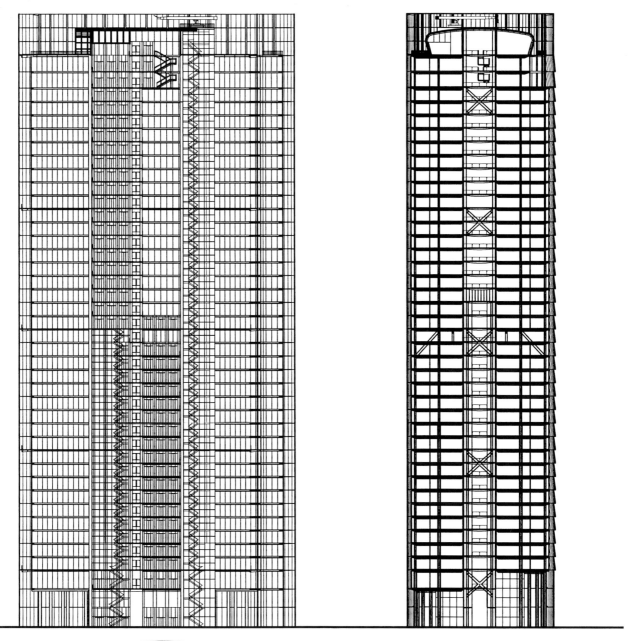

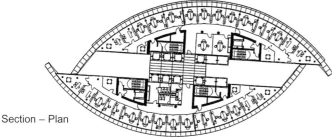

Section – Plan

0 5 10   20 M

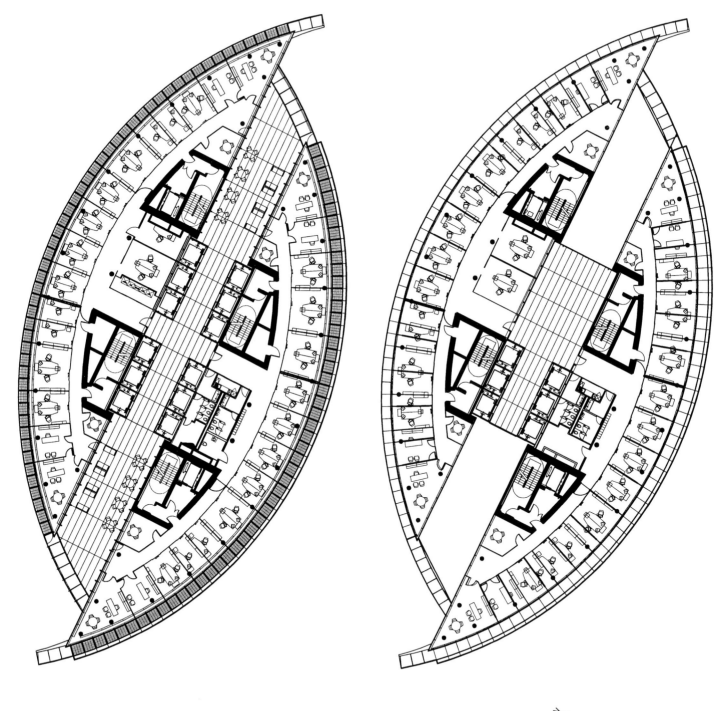

21st Floor – Skygarden

25th Floor – Typical Floor

N

0 2 4 6   10 M

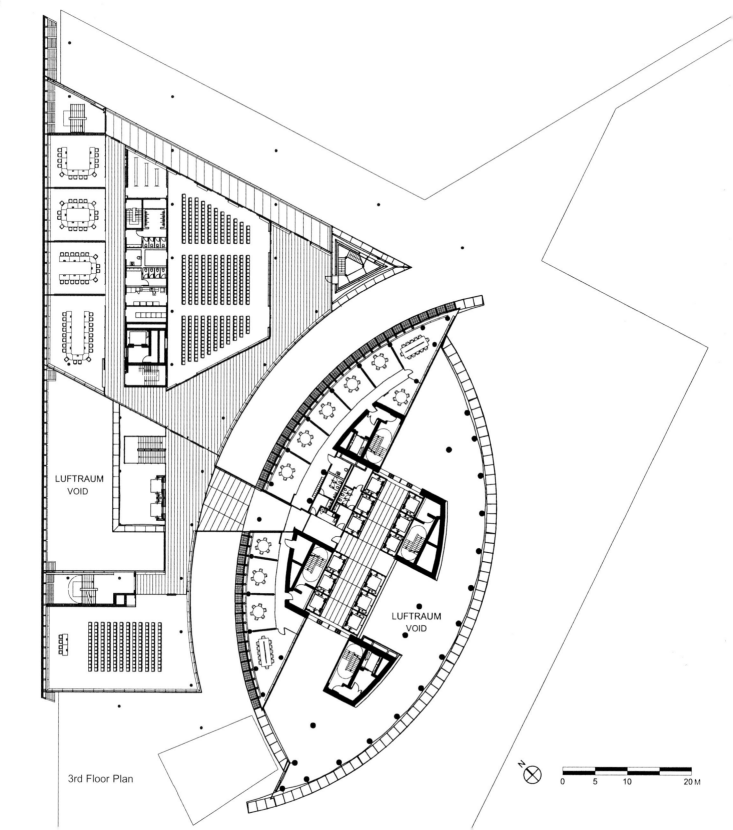

LUFTRAUM
VOID

LUFTRAUM
VOID

3rd Floor Plan

N

0   5   10   20 M

Gebäudehülle
Engineering und Technologie

Die zweischalige Hülle des Gebäudes ist ganz aus Glas. Struktur, Material und Konstruktion sind ablesbar – wie in einem klaren Diagramm. Die zweischalige Fassade ermöglicht die natürliche Belüftung der Büros, wann immer es die Außentemperatur – vor allem im Frühjahr und Herbst – erlaubt. Die äußere Haut gibt Schutz vor Regen, Wind und Lärm, und zugleich ist im Zwischenraum Platz für die Sonnenschutzjalousien. Die geschosshohen Glaswände optimieren das Tageslicht: Sonnenschutz und Licht sind automatisch gesteuert und kontrolliert. Vor allem im Sommer und im Winter schafft ein Quellluftsystem, unterstützt von einem Kühlungs- und Heizungselement, entlang der Fassade ausreichenden Komfort. Die zweischalige Fassade schafft so mit Hilfe minimaler Gebäudetechnik die optimalen und gewünschten Innenraumbedingungen. Dadurch werden beträchtliche Energieeinsparungen gegenüber einschaligen Fassaden erzielt. Die gläserne Außenhülle ist über das Gebäude hinaus erweitert und schafft in den beiden obersten Geschossen vor Wind und Wetter geschützte Dachgärten und Penthouse-Büros. Diese Hülle wird auch zum «Screen» für die Satellitenantennen. Sie werden damit ein Bestandteil der Ästhetik des Gebäudes, ohne dabei den klaren Abschluss der Gebäudehülle zu stören. Das Dach über dem Annex gleicht einer gekrümmten Fassade. Über dem Stahlraster sind adaptive Zellen angeordnet. Es dient als Dacheindeckung, Dämmung, Lärmschutz und ermöglicht Belüftung und den Einfall von natürlichem Tageslicht. Je nach Nutzungsanforderungen oder neu vorhandenen Technologien ist dieses System im Laufe der Lebenszeit des Gebäudes mit geringstem Aufwand austauschbar und anpassbar.

The Building Shell
Engineering and Technology

The building's twin-shell facade is made entirely out of glass. The structure, material, and design are all legible, as in a very clear diagram. The twin-shell facade enables natural ventilation of the offices whenever the outside temperature permits – primarily in spring and fall. The outer skin of the facade protects against rain, wind and noise, while sunscreens are located in the intermediate space. The story-high glass walls optimize natural light: sunscreen and light levels are controlled automatically. In winter and summer especially, a ventilation system reinforced by a heating-and-cooling component ensures comfort levels all along the interior facade. With a minimum of building technology, the twin-shell facade creates optimum, desired conditions in the building's interior. The energy-saving properties of this system are considerably greater than those of a single-shell facade. The external glass shell extends upwards past the top of the building and protects the rooftop gardens and penthouse offices on the top two floors against wind and bad weather. The shell likewise serves as a "screen" for satellite antennas, which are thereby converted into components of the building's aesthetic without disturbing the clear margin of the facade.

The roof over the annex and penthouse resembles a curved façade consisting of a cellular panel system covering a steel frame. These panels are roofing/insulation, acoustical protection, ventilation and daylight admitting, which can be adapted and changed with future technologies.

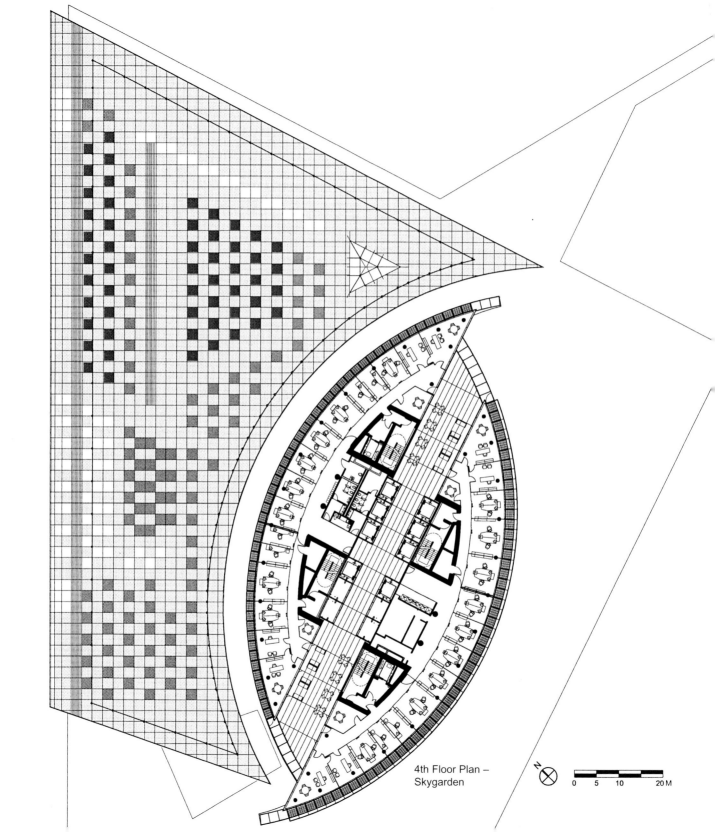

4th Floor Plan –
Skygarden

N

0   5   10   20 M

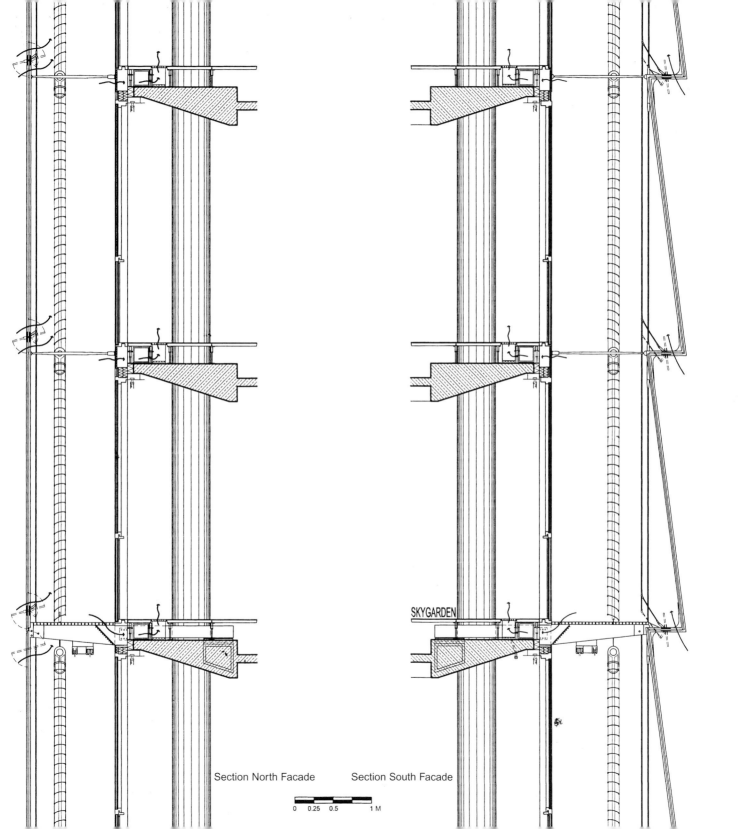

SKYGARDEN

Section North Facade   Section South Facade

0   0.25   0.5   1 M

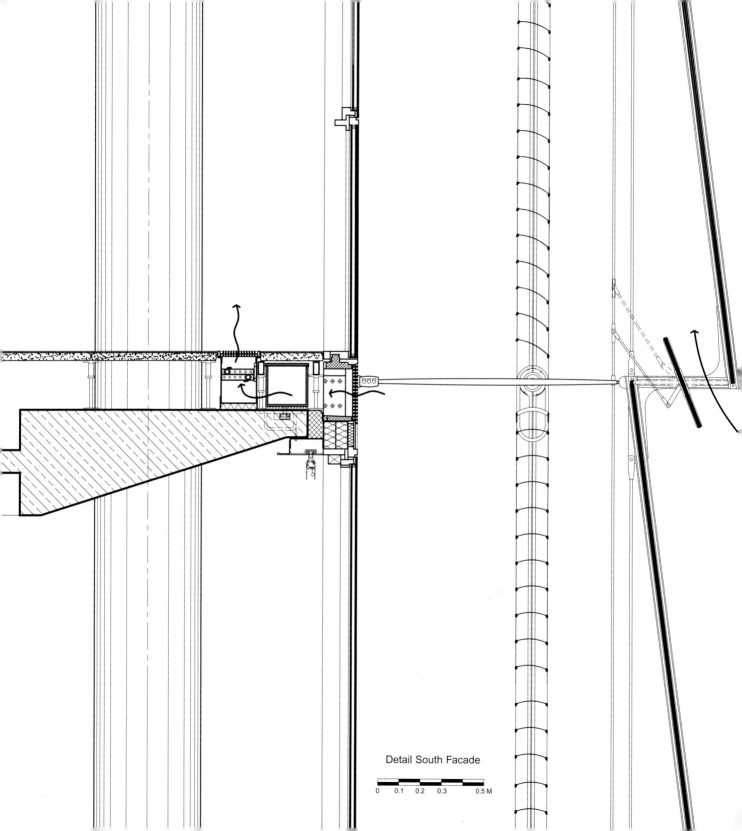

Detail South Facade

0   0.1   0.2   0.3   0.5 M

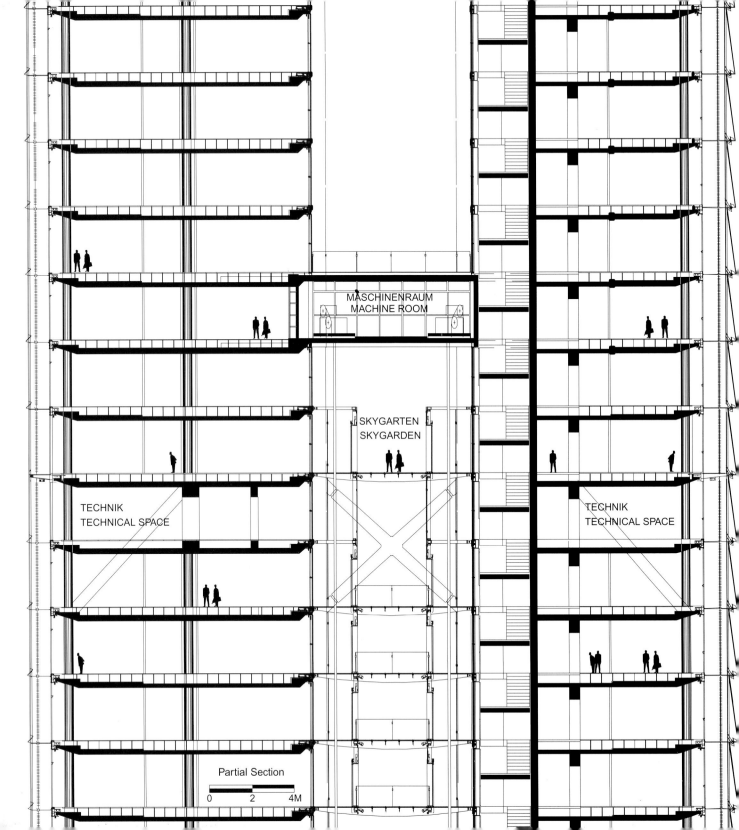

MASCHINENRAUM
MACHINE ROOM

SKYGARTEN
SKYGARDEN

TECHNIK
TECHNICAL SPACE

TECHNIK
TECHNICAL SPACE

Partial Section

0   2   4M

Innenraum
Maß und Transparenz

Das Erdgeschoss weist räumliche Großzügigkeit und Offenheit zum Rheinauen-Park auf. Von der Kurt-Schumacher-Straße im Westen oder der Autovorfahrt her im Osten betritt man die viergeschossige Halle im «Spalt» des Gebäudes mit direktem Zugang zu den Aufzügen. Diese Halle erweitert sich im Süden zu einem großzügigen Piano Nobile über dem Rheinauen Park. Die Nutzung ist flexibel für Ausstellungen, Empfänge oder Veranstaltungen. Die gebogene, überdachte Galleria trennt den Turm vom zweigeschossigen Annex. Hier sind Läden, Cafeteria und Restaurants untergebracht, die sich zum Park mit Terrassen öffnen. Von der Kurt-Schumacher-Straße aus ist ein Kurzzeitparkplatz erschlossen. Der landschaftsgestaltete Freiraum entlang dem «Schürmann-Bau» wird bis zum Eingang fortgesetzt. Im Nordflügel des Turms und im Annex sind das Konferenz- und Seminarzentrum und der große Vortragssaal untergebracht. Die Erschließung kreuzt hier Halle und Passage und ist dadurch offen, übersichtlich und erlebnisreich. Wie auf Stegen bewegt man sich über der Parklandschaft.

Die Formenvielfalt in der Architektur ist subjektiv, demgegenüber steht das Experimenthafte der objektiven Form. Es braucht eine selbstbewusste Sachlichkeit, um sich der konstruktiven Wahrheit zu nähern. In den beiden Bauwerken, dem Post Tower in Bonn und der Konzernzentrale Bayer in Leverkusen, ist aus dem Dreiklang Architekt, Ingenieur und Gebäudetechniker ein Einklang zwischen Gestalt und Technik geworden. Das Dazwischen – das «in between» – ist nicht Zufall, sondern eine bewusste Entwicklung, um Architektur wieder in den ursprünglichen Zusammenhang mit Form zu bringen. Dieses Projekt entstand als Zusammenarbeit zwischen Architekt Helmut Jahn und den Ingenieuren Werner Sobek und Matthias Schuler. Diese Zusammenarbeit hat zu einer neuen Lesbarkeit der Architektur geführt.

Gutes Bauen müsste sich wie die Natur aus ihren innewohnenden Kräften und Gesetzen entwickeln: Die Natur, das organisch Belebte, ist mit der Form, dem anorganischen Leblosen, in Verbindung zu bringen. Helmut Jahn hat uns mit seinem neuesten Werk in Bonn mit der Natur wieder zur Form hingeführt. Die gelungene Allegorie der Stille, die in der Eingangshalle herrscht, wurde zu einem kontemplativen Ort, wo Gebäude und Natur aus einer klaren Ordnung der Konstruktion zusammenkommen. Die Landschaft, die in das transparente Rauminnere dringt, schafft Wohlklang und erfüllt die Sehnsucht nach Schönheit.

The Interior
Measure and Transparency

The ground floor demonstrates considerable spaciousness and openness vis-a-vis the Rheinauen Park. From either Kurt-Schumacher-Strasse to the west or the car entrance ramp in the east, one enters the four-story main hall in the building's "split," where the elevators are located. This hall extends south into a spacious Piano Nobile over the park. The space is versatile and can be used for exhibits, receptions, and other public events. The well-designed, curved Galleria separates the tower from the two-story annex, which contains shops, a restaurant, and bistros with terraces opening out onto the park. Short-term parking is accessible from Kurt-Schumacher-Strasse. The landscaped open space along the "Schürmann Bau" extends up to the entrance. The conference and seminar center and the large lecture hall are all housed in the tower's north wing and in the annex. Here the route of access bisects both the hall and the passageway and is thus spacious, clearly defined, and open for activity. People move back and forth across the landscape of the park as if on footbridges.

The diversity of forms in architecture is subjective; set against it is the experimentality of objective form. Experimentality requires a confident realism in order to approximate the truth of design. In both the Post Tower in Bonn and the Bayer AG Corporate Headquarters in Leverkusen, a triad of architect, engineer, and building technician has created a unity of form and technology. This "in-betweenness" is no accident; rather, it involves a deliberate process of reinvoking architecture's original relationship to form. This project grew out of a collaboration between architect Helmut Jahn and engineers Werner Sobek and Matthias Schuler. The unity of their coordinated work has led to a new legibility in architecture.

Good building must develop, like nature, out of its own internal forces and laws: living, organic Nature must be brought into contact with lifeless, anorganic Form. With his most recent work in Bonn, Helmut Jahn has again given us form through nature. The effective allegories of silence predominating in the lobby create a contemplative place where structure and nature come together. The landscape permeating the interior creates harmony and fulfills the desire for beauty.

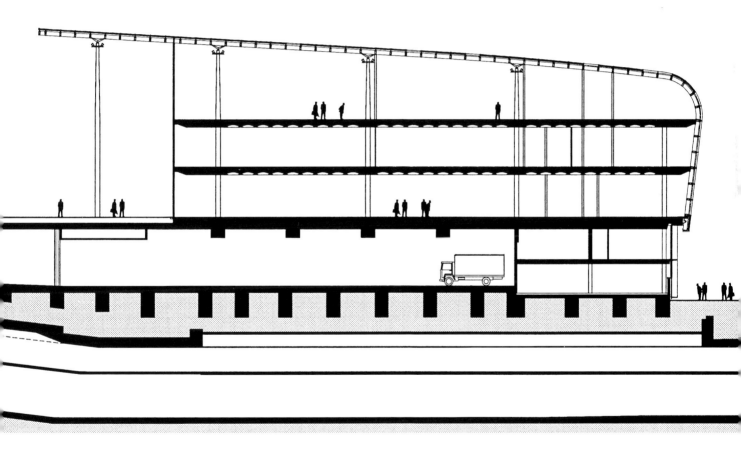

Section Base Building

0   5   10   20M

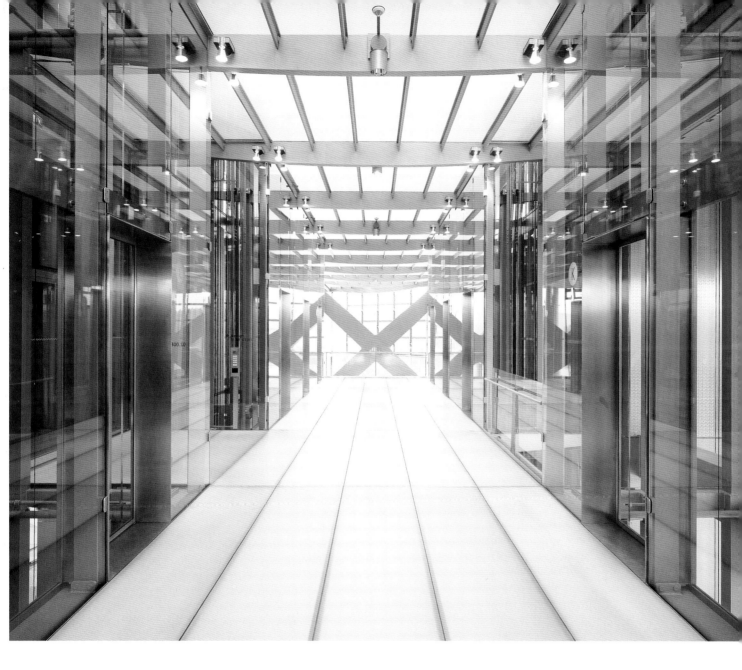

Technische Angaben / Technical Data

Hochhaus / Tower:

Gebäudehöhe / Building Height:
Glasfassade / Glass Facade 162.40 m
Dachebene / Roof Level 151.55 m

Geschosshöhe / Office Floor Height:
Büros / Offices 3.55 m
Erdgeschoss / Ground Floor 10.00–15.00 m
Skygärten / Skygardens 32.00 m

Ebenen / Levels:
1 Ebene Eingangshalle / 1 Lobby Level
1 Ebene Konferenzräume / 1 Level Conference Rooms
4 Skygärten / Skygardens
37 Ebenen Büros / 37 Levels Offices
1 Ebene Vorstandsbesprechungsräume (Penthouse) / 1 Level Executive Conference Area (Penthouse)
1 Technikgeschoss (20. OG) / 1 Level Mechanical (20th floor)
5 Ebenen Tiefgarage, Technik, Lager (UG) / 5 Levels Parking, Mechanical, Storage (UG)

Flächen / Areas:
Umfang / Circumference 179 m
Typische Bruttogeschossfläche Büroebene / Gross Floor Area Typical Office Floor: 1,534 m²
Typische Bruttogeschossfläche Skygartenebene / Gross Floor Area Typical Level Skygardens: 1,930 m²
Bruttogeschossfläche überirdisch / Gross Floor Area Above Ground: 65,323 m²

Basisgebäude / Base Building:

Gebäudehöhe (variierend) ca. / approx. Building Height (varying) 15.00–20.00 m
Geschosshöhe / Floor Height:
5.00 m 1. OG / First Conference Level / Ground Floor
5.00 m – 10.00 m 2. OG / Second Conference Level

Ebenen / Levels:
1 Ebene Restaurant, Ausstellung / 1 Level Restaurant, Exhibit
2 Ebene Konferenzräume / 2 Levels of Conference Rooms
1 Ebene Bibliothek, Konferenzzentrum, spezielle Nutzungen / 1 Level Library, Conference Center, Special Uses
1 Ebene Konferenzzentrum / 1 Level Conference Center

Geschossflächen / Floor Areas:
Bruttogeschossfläche Erdgeschoss /
Gross Floor Area Ground Floor: 2,240 m²
Bruttogeschossfläche 1. OG / Gross Floor Area First Level: 2,228 m²
Bruttogeschossfläche 2. OG / Gross Floor Area Second Level: 2,257 m²
Bruttogeschossfläche überirdisch / Gross Floor Area Above Ground: 6,726 m²

Untergeschosse / Lower Levels:

Parkplätze / Parking Spaces:
UG 2 / Lower Level 2:   56
UG 3 / Lower Level 3:   170
UG 4 / Lower Level 4:   170
UG 5 / Lower Level 5:   170
Gesamt / Total: 566

Am Bau Beteiligte / Names of Persons Involved

Bauherr / Client

Deutsche Post AG, Bonn
vertreten durch / represented by:
Deutsche Post Bauen GmbH
Geschäftsführer / Chief Executive Officer: Franz Werner Nolte
Projektleiter / Projekt Manager: Hans Peter Kröll

Architekt / Architect:

Murphy/Jahn, Inc.
Helmut Jahn, Sam Scaccia, Steven Cook, Gordon Beckman, Yorgo Lykourgiotis,
Oliver Henninger, Bo Nielsen, Ingo Jannek, Andreas Hell, Frank Weingardt,
Charles Bostick, John Manaves, Jürgen Schreyer, Andrea Seegers, Wolfgang
Scherer, Ronald Wulle, Wolfgang Bauer, Chris Berger, Scott Becker, Dieter Zabel

Tragwerk und Gebäudehülle /
Structure and Enclosure:

Werner Sobek Ingenieure GmbH
Werner Sobek, Wolfgang Sundermann, Sigurdur Gunnarsson, Holger Hinz,
Christoph Dengler, Heike Myland, Daniela Schlageter

Hock + Reinke
Hans Reinke, Thomas Wombacher, Thomas Schiel

Energie und Komfort /
Energy and Comfort:

Transsolar Energietechnik GmbH
Matthias Schuler, Stefanie Reuss, Michael Jurenka, Tobias Fiedler,
Friedmann Kik, Claus Twerdy

Technische Systeme /
Mechanical Systems:

Brandi Consult GmbH
Tibor Rákóczy, Heribert Etscheid, Michael Kistermann

Bauleitung / Site Architect:

Heinle, Wischer und Partner
Sieghard Rieger, Stefan Rohleder

Landschaftsgestaltung /
Landscape Architect:

Peter Walker & Partners
David Walker

Spezialgebiete/Specialty Consultants:

Projektleitung / Project Manager:	Prof. Weiss & Partner
Beleuchtung / Lighting Consultant:	L-Plan, Michael Rohde
Lichtkunst / Lighting Art:	AIK Expeditions Lumiere, Yann Kersalé
Fassade / Facade Consultant:	DS-Plan
Bauphysik / Building Physics:	Horstmann + Berger
Feuerschutz / Fire Safety Consultant:	BPK
Aufzüge / Elevator Consultant:	Jappsen + Stangier GmbH
Böden / Soils Engineer:	Jessberger + Partner
Assistenz Landschaftsgestaltung / Associate Landscape Architects:	Gottfried Hansjakob Wolfgang Roth

Biografische Notizen

Helmut Jahn

Geboren 1940 in Nürnberg. Architekturstudium an der Technischen Hochschule in München, dann am Illinois Institute of Technology in Chicago. Seit 1967 bei C.F. Murphy Associates, wo er 1973 Partner wurde. 1981 wurde das Büro in Murphy/Jahn unbenannt, und 1983 übernahm er das Büro ganz. Seit über dreißig Jahren verfolge ich den Aufstieg von Helmut Jahn als Architekt, Chefarchitekt und Firmeninhaber. Sein erstes selbständiges Werk, die Auraria Library in Denver, publizierte ich 1977 in «after Mies». Später entstanden die Bücher «Airports» 1991, «Transparenz» 1996 und «Architecture/Engineering» 2002, «Bayer Konzernzentrale» 2003, alle im Birkhäuser Verlag Basel–Boston–Berlin. Architektur war immer eine Kunst, die Visionen Gestalt gibt. Es gehört zur Architecture-Engineering-Partnerschaft mit realistischen Grundlagen, das Neue leidenschaftlich anzupacken. Insbesondere konnte Helmut Jahn sein Image eines «high-tech architect» durch die Partnerschaft mit den Ingenieuren in ein zeitgemäßes Image umwandeln, das seiner heutigen Realität entspricht.

Werner Sobek

Geboren 1953 in Aalen (Württemberg). Bauingenieur- und Architekturstudium an der Universität Stuttgart, mit Promotion zum Doktor-Ingenieur. 1991 Gründung seines Ingenieurbüros in Stuttgart und seit 1995 Professor an der Universität Stuttgart, Leiter des Instituts für leichte Flächentragwerke und des Zentrallabors des konstruktiven Ingenieurbaus. Aus seinem Werk ist 1999 das Buch «Werner Sobek: Art of Engineering/Ingenieur-Kunst» und 2001 die Monografie «R 128» mit Frank Heinlein entstanden.

Matthias Schuler

Geboren 1958 in Stuttgart, Abschluss 1987 als Diplom-Ingenieur an der Universität Stuttgart, danach Assistent am Institut für Thermodynamik und Wärmetechnik. 1992 Gründung der Transsolar GmbH für KlimaEngineering in Stuttgart, eines Technologie-Büros für energieeffizientes Bauen und Nutzkomfort in Gebautem. 2001 Gastprofessur an der Harvard University, Department of Architecture. Im 2003 bei Birkhäuser erscheinenden Band «Transsolar – KlimaEngineering» wird seine Arbeit ausführlich vorgestellt.

Biographical Notes

Helmut Jahn

Born in Nuremberg in 1940, architectural studies at the Technische Hochschule in Munich and later at the Illinois Institute of Technology in Chicago. Joined C.F. Murphy Associates in 1967, made a partner in 1973. In 1981 the firm was renamed Murphy/Jahn and in 1983 Jahn took control of the business. I have followed the rise of Helmut Jahn as architect, chief architect and CEO for more than thirty years. His first independent work, the Auraria Library in Denver, was presented in my book "After Mies" (1977). There followed a series of books on his work, all published by Birkhäuser Verlag (Basel, Boston and Berlin): "Airports" (1991), "Transparency" (1996) and "Architecture/Engineering" (2002), "Bayer Headquarters" (2003). Architecture has always been an art that lends visions a concrete form. Every architecture/engineering partnership with a foundation in reality must demonstrate a passion for innovation. Through his partnership with engineers, Helmut Jahn has been able to revamp his image as a "high-tech" architect, making it more contemporary and reflective of his current work.

Werner Sobek

Born in Aalen (Württemberg) in 1953, civil engineering and architectural studies at the University of Stuttgart, doctorate in engineering, 1991 establishment of his own engineering firm in Stuttgart, 1995 professorship at the University of Stuttgart, director of the Institut für Leichte Flächentragwerke and the Zentrallabor des Konstruktiven Ingenieurbaus. His work is described in the book "Werner Sobek: Art of Engineering/Ingenieur-Kunst" (1999) and the monograph "R 128", co-authored with Frank Heinlein (2001).

Matthias Schuler

Born in Stuttgart in 1958, master's degree in engineering in 1987 from the University of Stuttgart, lecturer at the Institut für Thermodynamik und Wärmetechnik. In 1992 Schuler founded Transsolar GmbH für Klima Engineering in Stuttgart, a technology company devoted to energy-efficient architecture and utilitarian comfort in buildings. 2001 visiting professorship at the Harvard University, Department of Architecture. The book "Transsolar – KlimaEngineering", which will be published by Birkhäuser in 2003, presents the company's work in detail.

Über den Autor

Werner Blaser, geboren 1924 in Basel, studierte nach einem Praktikum bei Alvar Aalto am Illinois Institute of Technology in Chicago, wo er unter anderem mit Mies van der Rohe in Kontakt trat. In eigenen Entwürfen, zahlreichen Ausstellungen und Architekturpublikationen über Ost-Europa, Japan und China sowie Monografien über seine Lehrmeister Aalto und Mies van der Rohe setzt er sich seit Jahren mit den Fragen und Prinzipien der Architektur auseinander. In Basel führt er ein eigenes Büro für Architektur, Möbeldesign und Publizistik.

About the Author

Born in Basel in 1924, Werner Blaser completed his practical training with Alvar Aalto and then continued his studies at the Illinois Institute of Technology in Chicago which brought him into contact with such figures as Mies van der Rohe. Original designs, numerous exhibitions and publications on Eastern Europe, Japan and China, as well as monographs on his mentors Aalto and Mies van der Rohe have, for years, been Blaser's means of confronting and analyzing architectural questions and tenets. Now heading his own firm in Basel, he is active as designer, architect and publicist.

Bücher über die Architekten/Ingenieure von Werner Blaser bei Birkhäuser/
Books available about the architects/engineers by Werner Blaser at Birkhäuser:

Bayer Konzernzentrale/Headquarters. Helmut Jahn – Werner Sobek – Matthias Schuler, 2003
Helmut Jahn – Architecture Engineering. Helmut Jahn – Werner Sobek – Matthias Schuler, 2002
Werner Sobek: Art of Engineering/Ingenieur-Kunst, 1999
R128 by Werner Sobek (Werner Blaser/Frank Heinlein), 2002